HE NEVER COMPLAINS

Sam and Xavier Hutchins:
A Father and Son's Journey with Autism

Coach Sam

For my son, Xavier Duran Hutchins,
whose life, legacy, and lessons continue
to guide me.

And for the autism community-
families, caregivers, and advocates-
your courage and strength inspire this work.

TABLE OF CONTENTS

ACKNOWLEDGMENTS

I would first like to honor the life and spirit of my son Xavier Duran Hutchins, your connection to me has changed my life, and its in your memory that these words find its deepest meaning.

To my wife, Dawn Cofer Hutchins, thank you for walking beside me with love and patience, even when you did not understand. To his sisters, Carlitha Hutchins and Talecia Hutchins, and to his younger brother Dante Hutchins. Thank you for each part that you played in his life, which helped carrying forward his light into the world.

My gratitude is extended to Janice Mack and Joyce Brown, for your kindness and steady support and love shown to my son and to Kenneth Lumpkin, whose encouragement gave me the final push to complete this book. Gladys Hutchins, thank you for always believing in me when I needed it the most.

To Sam and Gina Mitchell, Steve Jascewsky, and everyone at Autism Rocks and Rolls, and Bridget Wilson of the Hope 4 Xavier foundation, and to Jacquline for being a great mother, and to my pastor, Sylvania Watkins and his wife Lady Tracee Watkins as well as my church family at the Greater Breakthrough Christian ministries. Thank you for your prayers, your covering, and spiritual guidance.

To Nicholas Morrill, you are a man's man and a true friend, always encouraging me to be the best version of me, and a great mentor for me and my cause.

Thank you.

Above all, I give glory and honor to my Lord and Savior, Jesus Christ, who has kept me throughout my life, sustained me throughout the journey to share this story.

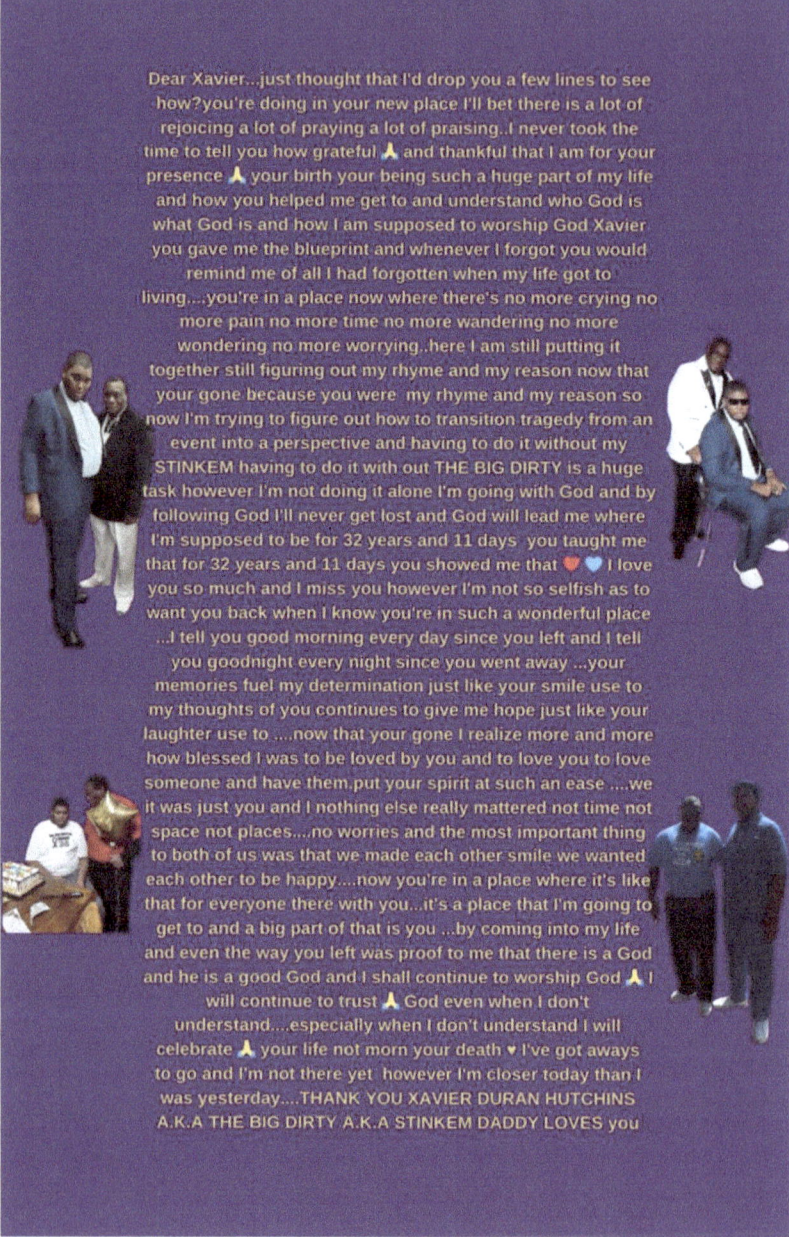

Dear Xavier...just thought that I'd drop you a few lines to see how?you're doing in your new place I'll bet there is a lot of rejoicing a lot of praying a lot of praising..I never took the time to tell you how grateful and thankful that I am for your presence your birth your being such a huge part of my life and how you helped me get to and understand who God is what God is and how I am supposed to worship God Xavier you gave me the blueprint and whenever I forgot you would remind me of all I had forgotten when my life got to living....you're in a place now where there's no more crying no more pain no more time no more wandering no more wondering no more worrying..here I am still putting it together still figuring out my rhyme and my reason now that your gone because you were my rhyme and my reason so now I'm trying to figure out how to transition tragedy from an event into a perspective and having to do it without my STINKEM having to do it with out THE BIG DIRTY is a huge task however I'm not doing it alone I'm going with God and by following God I'll never get lost and God will lead me where I'm supposed to be for 32 years and 11 days you taught me that for 32 years and 11 days you showed me that ❤️ 💙 I love you so much and I miss you however I'm not so selfish as to want you back when I know you're in such a wonderful place ...I tell you good morning every day since you left and I tell you goodnight every night since you went away ...your memories fuel my determination just like your smile use to my thoughts of you continues to give me hope just like your laughter use to ....now that your gone I realize more and more how blessed I was to be loved by you and to love you to love someone and have them put your spirit at such an ease ....we it was just you and I nothing else really mattered not time not space not places....no worries and the most important thing to both of us was that we made each other smile we wanted each other to be happy....now you're in a place where it's like that for everyone there with you...it's a place that I'm going to get to and a big part of that is you ...by coming into my life and even the way you left was proof to me that there is a God and he is a good God and I shall continue to worship God I will continue to trust God even when I don't understand....especially when I don't understand I will celebrate your life not morn your death ♥ I've got aways to go and I'm not there yet however I'm closer today than I was yesterday....THANK YOU XAVIER DURAN HUTCHINS A.K.A THE BIG DIRTY A.K.A STINKEM DADDY LOVES you

FOREWORD

James 1:2-4: *"Consider it pure joy, my brothers and sisters, whenever you face trials of many kinds, because you know that the testing of your faith produces perseverance."*

Resilience. Faith. Trust. If three words could describe the tale of Sam and Xavier's story it would be these mighty three. It is the development of resilience, the employment of faith, and the power of trust that is woven through every fiber of this father-son relationship. No matter the hurdles, no matter the tests resilience, faith, and trust continues to make this story one of great power and impact.

Sam tells a story of developing and delivering hope through this display of resilience, faith, and trust. His journey through a unique experience in parenting became not only a turning point in life bringing him closer to God but also helped shaped his ability to serve others through education, advocacy, love, and support. As a former ABA therapist, I understand the intensity, dedication, and patience involved in supporting a child with Autism. But, as a relative and supporter of the Hope for Xavier Foundation, I also know the power of unique passion that comes from a loving parent, blended with the knowledge and insight of a person devoted to making an impact.

He Never Complained: Sam and Xavier's Father and Son Journey with Autism gives you an inside glance into the trials, wins, and personal development experienced by all of Team Xavier. If anything, it is a testament to the fact that together we can accomplish so much and that you never know who your story…your life…may be inspiring.

Sam's focus on the importance of communication is a vital part of this work's message. Understanding that a child's receptive language can be strengthened through speech therapy despite their nonverbal status is crucial in developing functional communication with your autistic loved one. In expounding upon this key point, Sam provides families with keen knowledge to support what every loving family desires, despite the cognitive challenges of its members: healthy dynamics fostered by a shared level of communication.

It takes a certain degree of courage and strength to bleed one's truth via his pen…sprawled out on paper for all the world to take in, ponder, and analyze. I literally held my hand to my heart as I read Sam's account of losing that which he holds most dear to him: Xavier. I have always been of the mindset that our pain can fuel our passion and highlight our purpose. While this idea still feels valid, I would go even further to say that for Sam his present from God, Xavier, served to develop his passion and birth his purpose. The pain of the loss is an emotional and mental manifestation of the everlasting love for and bond with Xavier.

There is but one thing that our dear Sam got wrong in his text. When he stated, "I am not God" the slight error stood out to me because, without a doubt, it is the God in him that is at work as he continues to move mountains via the Hope 4 Xavier Foundation. Sam, the higher power you lean on is the very light that shines through you, through your work, through your efforts, and through your passion.

As the reader, I urge you to approach this text with an open heart and the readiness to learn. Whether you are a parent of an autistic individual, a supporter, a community support / mental health/ medical care provider, or a random community member, there is something to be learned within these pages. Knowledge is the keenest sense of power. I implore you to take what you learn here and end the bounds of gatekeeping by sharing it with someone else. Beyond that, I encourage you to also share any knowledge that you may have that can support another family or individual who is simply trying to build resiliency. Your hands on this book is not a mistake. It is part of a larger plan that you may never be privy to. Your charge is but to do your part by passing it on.

Resilience. Faith. Trust. May Xavier and Sam's narrative give you renewed belief in the power of resilience, faith, and trust.

Kenni York, MS, APC

-Author of Noah's Rights & Familial Sins

Dear Xavier...just thought that I'd drop you a few lines to see how you're doing in your new place. I'll bet there is a lot of rejoicing, a lot of praying, a lot of praising.

I never took the time to tell you how grateful and thankful that I am for your presence, your birth, your being such a huge part of my life and how you helped me get to and understand who God is, what God is, and how I am supposed to worship God. Xavier, you gave me the blueprint, and whenever I forgot, you would remind me of all I had forgotten when my life got to living.

You're in a place now where there's no more crying, no more pain, no more time, no more wandering, no more wondering, no more worrying. Here I am still putting it together, still figuring out my rhyme and my reason now that you're gone, because you were my rhyme and my reason. So now I'm trying to figure out how to transition tragedy from an event into a perspective, and having to do it without my STINKEM, having to do it without THE BIG DIRTY is a huge task. However, I'm not doing it alone. I'm going with God, and by following God, I'll never get lost, and God will lead me where I'm supposed to be. For 32 years and 11 days, you taught me that. For 32 years and 11 days, you showed me that.

I love you so much, and I miss you. However, I'm not so selfish as to want you back when I know you're in such a wonderful place. I tell you good morning every day since you left, and I tell you goodnight every night since you went away. Your memories fuel my determination just like your smile used to. My thoughts of you continue to give me hope, just like your laughter used to.

Now that you're gone, I realize more and more how blessed I was to be loved by you and to love you. To love someone and have them put your spirit at such an ease... it was just you and I, nothing else really mattered. Not time, not space, not places, no worries.

And the most important thing to both of us was that we made each other smile; we wanted each other to be happy.

Now you're in a place where it's like that for everyone there with you. It's a place that I'm going to get to, and a big part of that is you. By coming into my life and even the way you left was proof to me that there is a God, and he is a good God, and I shall continue to worship God. I will continue to trust God even when I don't understand, especially when I don't understand. I will celebrate your life, not mourn your death.

I've got always to go and I'm not there yet, however, I'm closer today than I was yesterday.

THANK YOU, XAVIER DURAN HUTCHINS A.K.A THE BIG DIRTY A.K.A STINKEM. DADDY LOVES you.

Chapter 1

Xperince getting prepared for the life ahead

This story starts on February 4th, 1962, at around 11 AM in a hospital called Button Gwinnett in Lawrenceville, Georgia, when I, Samuel Duran Hutchins, was born to Samuel and Mary M. Hutchins. I was the first of four boys born into the family, which, by all accounts (unknowingly at the time), put me in a de facto role as a leader. This would serve me well in my life later. I was the big brother, the standard by which all of my siblings behind me would be judged. Again, I didn't know this then, but would come to the realization later on.

My first memories of my childhood would begin around two years old. I was an only child at the time; however, my younger brother and second-born, Dale, was, as we say, a "bun in the oven," or simply put, my mom was pregnant with Dale, but I digress. My mom and dad went into the supermarket, and I was left alone in the care of my grandmother, Eunice Chandler, who, according to legend, was crazy about me as a child, as I was her fourth grandchild on that side of the family. According to her, I could read at the age of two. Again, this is according to her; I mean, I was there too, however, you have to keep in mind that I'm two. So, she says that I started reading the writing on the store window. If you remember back in the 1960s, there was this particular brand of detergent called TIDE, and there was a commercial with a jingle that went something like this: "Dirt can't hide from Intensified Tide." My grandmother said that I started repeating this jingle and spelling out the letters from across the street, and she couldn't see where I was getting what I was saying from. I said, "Look, Grandma," and as I pointed in the general direction, she saw where it was coming from, and she said she was amazed. When my mom and dad returned, she informed them first by asking, "Did you all know that this child can read?" And she had me do it again for them, which I did, and while they were impressed, it was to a lesser degree than my grandmother was. It still became a story for the ages, mine anyway.

I was always a child who had a sense of fair play and believed that doing the right thing was very important, even when no one was looking. I believed that cheating was wrong, and when I got cheated, I felt really bad and wondered why and how could people be okay with that. But as I've learned as an adult, children who grow up thinking it's okay to cheat become adults who think it's okay to rob, steal, and cheat, changing their trajectory in life and to a degree, the families that they create and the environment that they live in.

My sense of fairness would serve me well as I grew into an eight-year-old. We had two corner stores, and older ladies in the neighborhood would ask the kids to go to the store for them. They would give you a quarter or a dime, which, back in 1970, for an eight-year-old, was a lot of money because there was such a variety of penny candy. For a quarter, you got a sack full of candy—ah, yes, a simpler time.

I became in popular demand among the older ladies to run their store errands, and I didn't know why until later in life. When I was around twenty or twenty-one years old, I asked one lady in particular why she always asked me to do her store errands for her. She said, "Because you always brought back the correct change, you didn't steal anything, and you came right back. You were just as happy to get a dime as you were a quarter, and sometimes I could tell you, 'I'll pay you later' or 'set you up later,' and you would say okay." As it turned out, all of them felt the same way, and this came at a time when I had only four months before I found my dad dead on the way to school.

Now you have to understand, my dad was my hero. He was funny, a hard worker, somewhat of a jokester, and he also drank on the weekends, which sometimes accounted for some domestic violence between my mother and my father. Now, before you start judging my father, as I'm sure some of you instantly have, my mother was dishing out her fair share, too. You see, they both had issues of infidelity, which caused a lot of instability in our family dynamic. I didn't go to the same school for a whole year until he died, which will lead me to tell you all about my father's death, which has turned out to be the first of four scars on my heart that won't heal, and it has been there the longest.

The timeline: March 3rd, 1970, approximately 6 AM. I was awakened by my mom to get ready to go to school. Just outside my window, or should I say our window, where my brothers and I slept (all four of us in one bed: my brother Alex and Dale on one end, my younger brother and I on the other), I heard my dad's car still running. It was very cold, and normally, he would be gone before I got up to start his workday, because he had to pick up workers who rode to work with him, around three to four guys who didn't have a car. So my mom was under the assumption that he had fallen asleep in his car and had overslept. I was told by my mom to go wake him up, as she would say to me, "He should have already been gone to work."

So my first trip out there, I opened the door—yes, it was unlocked—and I started to shake him, and he did not awaken. So I go back in the house and tell my mom, "He won't wake up." And she sends me back out there with the instruction to shake him harder. I go back out to the car, get in, and proceed to shake him harder per my mother's instructions. Same result. So I go back in and let her know that he still won't wake up. So I was instructed by my mom to go try it again, the third time, and for the third time, same result. So I go back in the house, tell her again. This time she says, "Let me go wake him up, he's probably playing possum." And the next sound that I heard was a blood-curdling scream that I will never forget, and I heard a similar scream later in life when the first scar that will not heal was placed in my life and in my heart.

The next thing I know is the yard had police, sheriff, fire engines, ambulance, lights, sirens blaring. And then I was told a couple of days later that my hero was gone. He was dead. The cause of death was carbon monoxide poisoning, and just like that, my life was changed forever. Who I was to become, and who I was to be, and the kind of person I was to become, was formed.

That day, you could say the dye was cast. That day, my temperament, my calmness, my "never get too high, never get too low" philosophy came from this one event. Grief counseling was nonexistent in the Black community then, so childhood grief counseling was unheard of.

I was my dad's first son. Some of his and my mom's arguments would be about him taking me with him and coming back drunk. I remember him sitting me up on the bar while he drank and laughed; I always remembered people around him were always laughing. He was a huge Temptations fan and thought David Ruffin was the greatest singer of all time. As I stated earlier in this chapter, I had a knack for jingles, and it carried over into songs. My dad had a cassette player, and he had me memorize his favorite Temptations songs and sing them to his friends on the weekend. On the weekends they didn't come, he would be my only audience, and I just sang to him.

And now he's gone. No explanation, no rhyme, no reason. One thing about innocence, it can give you hope; it can disregard logic and make you think that the impossible is nonexistent. I had this thing in my head that when I went by the funeral home and saw my dad lying there, that when no one was looking, I would give him mouth-to-mouth resuscitation, and he would be alive again. This planted the seed for me that I would always have hope, no matter how grim logic tells me a situation is. I still try. It was now in me. "Death comes equally to us all, making us all equal" – John Donne, one of the most profound statements from one of my favorite poems, "For Whom the Bell Tolls." So, my sense of right and wrong and the importance of doing right and never condoning wrong, a sense of morality having an effect on me, was instilled with life lessons learned at an early age and enhanced as I grew older.

These are some of the events and life lessons that played a very important role in me becoming who I am and why I am the way I am. Be it right, wrong, or indifferent, all of this, as far as I am concerned, is God's plan.

The birth of Xavier and the initial joys and challenges of early parenthood. Sam's initial observations of Xavier's development and subtle hints of differences.

There were events that happened in my life leading up to the birth of my son, Xavier Duran Hutchins, also known as "The Big Dirty," "Big," "Zay," and "Stinkem," which made the timing of his birth so important and timely. You know how, when you reflect upon certain events in your life, you find yourself wondering why you remember a certain time or place when, at the time, it seemed so insignificant? And then, in retrospect and reflection, it was part of something that was preparing you for an event that would come later in life, and it would aid and assist you in whatever it is that you were chosen to do. The passion that you have meets the purpose, and the two entities join forces to drive you to the understanding of why you are here on God's Earth, and you understand it's God's Earth, so the purpose is also for God.

In saying that, let's go back to 1972. The death of my father did not totally end our nomadic tendencies for long. We spent a year living in the Glenwood Projects, apartment number 6. I was a huge fan of Batman, Superman, and Ultraman, and I was subliminally getting more induced, hypnotized, indoctrinated into truth, justice, and the American way—good triumphing over evil, and being the good guy was always my goal.

After that year and a couple more times moving, in 1972, we moved to a rural area called Tanners Bridge. We lived in front of a neighbor; their names were Jack and Frances Ellington. They had a son whose name was also Jack Ellington. I can't say if he was a Junior or not, but they called him "Baby Jack." Now, by today's standards, Baby Jack would have been diagnosed with autism. He had all of the classic signs, like rocking back and forth, hand flapping (except he would move his arms back and forth and clap his hands), and his vocabulary was limited, yet he always seemed happy—an accomplishment that years later was no small feat.

On this particular day, Mr. Jack Ellington was outside giving Baby Jack a shave, as Baby Jack couldn't do it himself. My friends and I went to see Baby Jack getting a shave. There were six of my friends, which made seven, including me. Now, bear in mind, Baby Jack had kind of a pointy nose, so to shave his upper lip, Mr. Jack Ellington had to raise his nose up to accomplish this. It made my other friends laugh, but for some reason, I didn't find it as amusing as my friends did. Instead, I focused on Mr. Jack Ellington's temperament and his demeanor, as he was taking his time, seeming only slightly annoyed by my friends' laughter, but it was trumped by the happiness displayed by the smile on Baby Jack's face. For the rest of my life before Xavier's birth, I would revisit that memory and wonder to myself, "Why do I remember that after all these years?"

My answer was on down the road, around 1974, when we moved again for the last time, which made this different: my mom had remarried, I got baptized, and was going to Whistleville Christian Church on the regular. It was a predominantly white church that had made the decision to integrate. And while I enjoyed a lot of great times there, around 1978, my belief in God disappeared. There were some events and people who pushed me in that direction, and all I will say about it at this time is: Racism is an evil and vile thing to have as part of your DNA in any capacity. In full disclosure and to be totally transparent, I also had a hand in it too.

So let's jump to September 7th, 1991. This is the time that I received the second scar that will not heal. It was the death of my mother. She was just forty-seven years old, and she used to joke with me about never having facial hair (I was the oldest, and yet all of my brothers were shaving, and she would sing to me...).

"BABYFACE YOU'VE GOT THE CUTEST LITTLE BABY FACE." She got such a kick out of that, and the second one was my age; she would always ask why was it taking me so long to turn 30 years old. She passed five months before I turned 30 years old. My mother was so very protective of me, and at the same time, she had higher expectations for me, in my mind, I let her down, and it haunts me to this day.

During our time of bereavement, I leaned on my grandfather, Amos Hutchins. He was mentally, and if you asked him, physically, the strongest man I knew. He always knew what to say and always even-keeled, and he really helped me through the grieving process with my mom. His talks and observations, and life lessons taught me things that continue to serve me to this day. You see, my grandfather and my mom were the two biggest influences in my life. And then, eleven months after my mom passed, Amos Hutchins died from stomach cancer at the age of 79, becoming the third scar that will not heal and placed on my heart and in my life.

Needless to say, I was in a depressed state of mind—one bad decision after another, a rudderless boat. I had no direction. And then, on November 16th, 1992, at approximately 10:30 PM on a Monday night, a 9-pound, 14-ounce, 21-inch long baby boy was born. Xavier Duran Hutchins said hello to the world. He was my third child: happy, handsome, and heavy. And it started my life on a journey that I didn't think I was ready for, but in reflection, I realize that God had been preparing me for this moment all my life.

His first year was so amazing. He could walk at 8 months, and as a 1-year-old, he was so much bigger than your typical one-year-old; he was wearing clothes the size of a 4-year-old. Life was good. I got a kick out of the look on people's faces when I told them he was only a year old, and those looks would come all the way through high school.

I came home from work one day, and his mother expressed to me that she had some concern about his communication skills and his social skills, none of which I could see. Because when I came through the door, he would always recognize that I was in the room, and when he could walk, he would greet me at the door. He paid so much attention to me and my actions to the point he would take my hand, lead me to the couch where I always sit. He would take the remote from whoever had the remote and change the channel to ESPN because he knew that's what I would do every day, and he would sit beside me and never move until I moved. We had a tradition where we would nose kiss like

Eskimos, and he never got tired of those. Whenever he got hurt or a band-aid was placed on him, at the end, he wanted his nose kiss. And the thing of it is, he had zero interest in sports of any kind; he just wanted to be near me. If someone else was sitting beside me on the couch, he would always try to squeeze in between that person and me. I always found this to be so funny, and he thought no one but him should sit in my lap, even when he grew to be 5 feet 8 inches and weighed 225 pounds at age 11, and those unpredictable growth spurts.

Now, mind you, Xavier and I wore the same size shoe when he was 11: size 9 and a half. So we went to a shoe store called Shoe Carnival Outlet, and they were having a shoe sale: buy one pair, get the second pair for half price. I'm looking and said in my head, "What a sale!" So I got he and I four pairs of shoes apiece. I called myself getting ahead of the game. So a month later, I'm trying to put on a pair of the new shoes, and none of them fit. His feet had grown from a size 9 and a half to a size 12, which blew my mind, and it wouldn't be the last.

November 23rd, 1994. This was the day of Xavier's first diagnosis. Before he was officially diagnosed with autism, his condition was called PDD, which is an acronym for Pervasive Developmental Disorder, which at the time was the diagnosis that was given to patients who displayed some signs of autism yet displayed abilities that said if they are autistic, then they should not have "this" ability. So we went with the PDD diagnosis for approximately two years, and then it was called ASD or Autism Spectrum Disorder. Now, prior to the ASD, I had dove headfirst into trying to find out everything I could about autism—movies, books, newspaper articles—because in the initial diagnosis, autism was mentioned. So I prepared myself as best I could to increase my knowledge of what it was that I was against and formulate a plan to give my son the best quality of life that I could. This became my mission. My life had taken a turn that I didn't see coming, and everything about my life and what was important was about to be rearranged. Team Xavier was in go mode, and failure was not an option.

Chapter 2

Xtraordinary journey begins

The HOPE 4 XAVIER FOUNDATION is an autism awareness organization inspired by my son, Xavier Duran Hutchins, also known as "The Big Dirty," "Big," "Zay," and "Stinkem." It started in July of 2015 with a group of parent-led advocates. We all had similar stories, and though our paths were different, they led us to a restaurant on a Saturday evening. There, we proclaimed and laid the groundwork for the HOPE 4 XAVIER FOUNDATION.

Although it was a community-friendly organization, we all felt (at the time, anyway) that we would be providing a valuable service to our community. Autism wasn't just a cause for us; it was personal. Everyone in the group, in its early stages, had a child with autism or was a caregiver, making autism a part of our daily lives. Unlike my other non-profit, DREAM OUTLOUD 2000, which was something I could put down and pick up, this was personal for all of us—or so I thought.

As it turns out, some people's passion, no matter how personal, comes at a price that some are unwilling to pay. They say a lot of things in a meeting that sound good at the time; however, when the "rubber meets the road," as they say, things can go south in a hurry. I think sometimes people say things because they're captured by the moment. The moment you have to put your passion into action, the moment you have to put your words into action, you find out pretty quickly who is genuinely in it with you and who is in it conditionally. As soon as that condition arises, you discover the very nature of who they are, and that once the excitement of the cause is gone, so are some peopls.

Needless to say, we lost three people after the first meeting. Why, I don't know; I never asked. We started with a total of twenty people, counting the children who were on the spectrum.

There was a member who was a single mom, and she had a son with autism and a daughter with ADHD. She was very strong in character, worked incredibly hard, and did the best she could. She wanted what we all initially wanted, and I understood that. For most of them, this was their first time in an organization, so they didn't understand how their passion should be connected to our objectives and purpose, or how collectively we could achieve great things.

Our plan was to raise money for research, create support groups, and provide experiences for our children. In our case, the school system would actually try to exclude Xavier from things like field trips and school outings because of his size. The thinking was, "What if he has a behavioral issue and it escalates into something we really don't want to deal with?" They would even send notes home asking if we could keep him home for field trips and school outings. We said, "Absolutely not!" Our reply was that I would come and accompany him on these school trips and outings. The problem I had with that was they were denying my son an opportunity, and that assumption was always an issue for me.

That Xavier could not do things, and we as parents could not allow this. All I want is for my son to have a chance. To exclude him just because you don't think he is capable is unacceptable. My position is this: give him a chance. If he can't, then I'm okay with other alternatives, like what I suggested—I would come and be his chaperone. My son is capable of some amazing things, some of which I didn't even know.

What I've come to learn with Xavier is that, given the chance, he will surprise you. Given the chance, he will succeed, and you will miss the opportunity to witness his greatness. You will miss the chance to witness a six-foot-four-inch, three-hundred-and-forty-eight-pound angel/miracle. To personally be a part of this journey is something I cherish and value. All the value he has

19

brought not just to my life, but to the lives of any and everyone who crosses his path, is immense.

We, as his family, could not sit idly by and have his chance to experience life without restriction, without prejudice. That became our goal at Team Xavier. We live to see him smile; we live to hear him laughing. His ability to just change people's mood when he decided to interact with you or what was going on is incredible.

Him and I playing "chase" is something that always brings a smile to my face. He would always run to me and make a growling noise. As soon as I make contact with him, he turns and, with this slow trot, runs toward his bedroom and jumps on the bed, waiting for me to come and tickle him and to hear me say, "I gotcha!" We would repeat this for the next twenty minutes until both of us would be tired. He would do something similar with his mom. She had a hard time hiding snacks from him because he had this uncanny knack for finding them no matter what. It would become his mission to sneak around until he found them, grab them, and head to his room. He rarely got caught.

But in the event that Xavier did get caught, he had two places of refuge to run to. One place of refuge was under his bed, and it would be so funny to come home and hear his mom trying to get him to come out. She'd actually try to run him out from under the bed by poking a broom under it, to no avail. This always had me in stitches because I would ask, "How long has he been under the bed?" If she said twenty minutes or longer, I would just laugh. With him hearing my voice, I would say, "BIG, COME OUT FROM UNDER THE BED!" He would roll out and quickly get behind me because, in his mind, "nothing is going to happen to me now, my daddy is here." His mom would tell him, "I'm still going to get you," and I would ask, just for giggles, what he had done. She would say what I already knew: he had found the snack stash and raided it.

This place of refuge worked for a while; however, he got so big he couldn't get under the bed fast enough. When I would come home, he'd have this look on his face—he was mad. I would ask him, "What's wrong, STINKEM?" He would get off the bed and take my hand. He and I would walk toward his mother, and he would take my hand and gesture as if he wanted me to hit her. This made me laugh as well. So, of course, Xavier and I would be on our way to a convenience store to get him a "goody bag," as it came to be known.

Now, his second place of refuge was the neighbor's house, who lived about two hundred feet away from Xavier's house. So, if he got caught in the act, he would high-tail it over to the neighbor's house. The lady's name was Janice, and she let Xavier get away with anything, sort of like me. I learned this one day when I came home and he was not there. Upon my inquiring of his whereabouts, I was informed that he was over at Janice's house. He ran over there because I had caught him trying to raid the snack stash again, and of course, she vowed to get him.

When he came back, I walked next door to Janice's house. Xavier saw me and made a beeline for me, but instead of leaving, he guided me to sit down. Now, Janice and I were classmates; we went to school together since seventh grade and graduated high school the same year. So, we were what you could call friends, and she was a huge fan of Xavier.

On this particular day, after he escorted me, or rather, instructed me, to sit down because he wasn't ready to go, Janice and I started a conversation about Xavier and how she calls him "her big baby." While we were carrying on the conversation, Xavier climbed up on the kitchen counter where there were shelves. Seeing this, I said to Xavier, "Zay, get down from there!" and I was quickly instructed to leave him alone—"He knows what he is doing."

Xavier got down a box of cereal and went to the dish rack on the other side of the counter and got a bowl. Then, he went into the refrigerator and got the milk out. I watched with my mouth open as he completed the task. After she told me to close my mouth, I asked Janice, "I didn't know he could do that!" She said, "Because y'all will not let him!" She explained the first time he did it, she was nervous too, but she stayed close in case he fell because he was seven years old when he first did it. She said he had been doing it ever since. Sometimes it's cereal, sometimes it's chips; she said he knows where everything is. This particular time, he was twelve years old, so he had been doing this for five years. Janice, like me, just let Xavier do what he does.

This was when I realized that even though Xavier is non-verbal, continuing the speech therapy was bridging the communication gap. It was evident that he could figure out what to do and how to do it on his own terms. Given the opportunity, the possibilities are endless. I escorted Xavier to his junior and senior prom. Xavier danced, laughed; he even unveiled his own signature dance called "The Big Dirty Shuffle."

It will always be about giving Xavier a chance and making sure he has that chance, not just in school but in life as well. We, as Team Xavier, will not allow any institution—be it school, church, restaurant, or any person—to place limitations on what Xavier can or cannot do. This was proven to me on that day: Xavier knows his limitations, and if you pay attention, he will show you what they are and what they are not.

There are a lot of strategies and plans in place to cope with the vast array of different situations that exist on the autism spectrum. While it can be very confusing without help, and in some cases a headache or even a nightmare, you cannot put off dealing with what is real and right in front of you. This is especially true if you take the attitude or approach that your person or your child will "grow out of it" or "grow into it," depending on your perception or perspective.

Let me tell you, and this is not just my opinion but my lived experience, not only with Xavier but also with people I've come in contact with and had extensive interaction with—parents and caregivers who have sought me out. As I found out, in our community, my son Xavier had become the face of autism. Xavier and Team Xavier have heightened awareness about autism. Without us even looking, we had no idea that Xavier and his situation were gaining so much attention. Xavier was being viewed as a success story; people were looking at Xavier as a goal, a sign of hope.

So, we would get questions on things like: "How do you get him to sit still for a haircut?" or "How do you get Xavier to sit still for three hours in a movie?" and "How is Xavier when you go to a restaurant?" We then started to realize that this was information we had and were only getting out to people who knew us, not understanding that there were people who had questions but didn't know us. However, they wanted that information, they needed that information, and for whatever reason, did not know how to get in touch with us or didn't know anyone who knew us.

The thing is, when people asked about those situations—like the haircuts, the movies, the restaurants, and his calm demeanor, and how happy he always seems to be—the answer to most of those questions was, and still is, EARLY INTERVENTION. Xavier was diagnosed at the age of two through a program called "Babies Can't Wait." It is the biggest reason that Xavier has the quality of life that people see. We stuck with the speech therapy even though he is non-verbal; it helped us and him to develop the communication that allowed us to understand Xavier.

Here's your paragraph with the grammatical errors and punctuation issues fixed, focusing on the unconventional understanding of success in autism therapy:

And it also aided in Xavier's learning to understand us. Even though this didn't lead to Xavier having or building a great verbal vocabulary, it did help Xavier and us develop understanding. And that's the thing you have to be careful of when you try to measure the success of therapies by what you see. For instance, it would be easy to conclude that speech therapy wasn't working because he wasn't speaking; his vocabulary wasn't increasing. Had we followed that logic, we would have been wrong as sin on Sunday.

You see, the things that you would normally measure success or failure by do not apply here. It wasn't about Xavier speaking or growing a thirty-word vocabulary, even though logically these should be the metrics which conventional thinking would call for us to measure success by. Given a certain amount of time, one could see where the conclusion would be drawn to give up on speech therapy because logic and those metrics would point you in that direction. However, that is part of the riddle: success on the spectrum comes in unconventional forms. A deeper understanding and patience have to be formed, and in some cases, summoned from within you. The ability to see and listen with your heart is crucial, so that you can see the hope that is there. But you will never see it as you should if you don't develop this unique ability.

Because we paid attention, and so was Xavier, we paid attention to how the speech therapist was teaching him word association. For example, they taught Xavier the difference between a fork and a spoon. This took him about a month, and of course, we were happy at the session when Xavier did it. So, a couple of days later, when we got home, Xavier and I were sitting on the couch. I had come from the kitchen and realized I had forgotten my spoon. Of course, my mind went back to the speech therapy session, and I said to myself, "Let's see if it was a coincidence or does Xavier really know the difference between a fork and a spoon?" So, I looked at him and said, "STINKEM, GO GET ME A SPOON."

Xavier got up, went into the kitchen, and I could hear the kitchen drawer opening and the rattling of utensils. When he emerged from the kitchen with a spoon, a smile quickly came across my face. As Xavier handed me the spoon, I grabbed and hugged him. I asked him for a kiss, and he laid one on my jaw. It was at this moment that I realized how successful the speech therapy was and that we, as Team Xavier, were on the right track.

So, what we learned was that speech therapy isn't just about building a vocabulary, although logic and conventional thinking would commonly lead you to think that way. No, the goal was communication. And if there is one thing that we learned, it's that success on the spectrum, while useful to all, is sometimes only understood as it should be by people on the spectrum. This "thinking outside the box"—going against conventional and logical thinking—can sometimes mislead people who cling to their conventional common sense and not allow them to see the success.

That is right in front of them, and this approach served us well in his ABA therapy, which led to calming Xavier down so we could attend a three-hour movie without interruption. We could go to a restaurant without incident, and all of this started at the age of two. By the time Xavier was eight years old, all of his "bad" behavior—or as we like to call it, his untimely behavior—was gone and almost nonexistent. This was because we recognized that there were some things or forces at work that if you are not in it, you would have a hard time seeing. Two of those things were early intervention and trust, which was becoming an even bigger factor in aiding Xavier with his communication skills and how he approached life and his perception of his life experiences.

Since he has more trust in me than anyone else on Team Xavier, this was important because with me, he knows that no harm is coming to him. He knows and feels that things are better when he sees me. He knows that whatever he has been wanting and has not been getting, he is going to get it, and all he has to do is let it be known to me, and he will get it because he already believes that. And isn't that the way we are supposed to be when it comes to our faith in God? Isn't that the instruction given by God in the Bible? God said, "Ask and it shall be given to you; seek and you shall find; knock and the door shall be opened." Xavier reinforced this for me, and he never read the Bible.

Again, you have to really pay attention to see how things are connected. Xavier and his communication, his ability to transition from one event to the next, his willingness to go places he had never been or do things he had never done were all connected to the element of trust. And the element of trust that he has in me is like that of or in no one else. Because of that, Xavier and I have this special relationship. It inspires, it uplifts, it encourages, and above all else, it gives hope. It is a divine relationship; it has been my saving grace. It is the reason that I am now heaven-bound. I can without a doubt say this, and to borrow a line from a gospel hymn, "I am working for my soul's salvation."

All of this—I mean everything—is all in God's plan. It is in God's hand, and it is all in God's time. Because God gave me time, God gave me grace, God gave me mercy, God gave me patience,

God gave me tolerance. God gave me Xavier. And in doing all of this for me, I now realize that I owe it to and I am thankful to God Almighty, the Great I Am, for loving me, for giving me my son, Xavier Duran Hutchins, "The Big Dirty," "Big," "Zay." And when it's just Xavier and I, he is my "Stinkem." I am now a blessed man. I am a man who has a passion and a purpose. Before, I was just a person with a passion and no purpose. And all of this changed when Xavier came into our lives, specifically when he came into my life. His life, his existence, is proof to me of the presence of God.

And now, things mean more to me. Doing a good thing means so much more to me because I now know and realize that doing good, doing what's right, and serving others is pleasing to God and it is pleasing in God's sight. And this is all because God knows who we are, God knows what we need, and God knew that I needed Xavier, and He blessed me with this living, breathing miracle. And I just want to thank you, Lord.

Chapter 3

Xtraordinary effects and efforts

The journey of understanding the autism spectrum can be many things: difficult, confusing, overwhelming, frustrating. It can be one of these, or it can be all of these. But one thing is for sure, it will reveal what's within you. It will let you know if you have what it takes to embark on and embrace wherever this journey is about to take you. It will reveal the kind of person you are, having you ask questions you never thought you'd ask and go to places you never imagined you would. You will discover how important and necessary it is to believe in a higher power. Your faith will need to be of such a nature that it continues to grow with you as you go on this journey, because you are going to have to believe in something, or in this case, someone greater than yourself. And for me, without question, that is my Lord and Savior Jesus Christ, the Son of the one and only true living God.

When I reflect back on how I doubted that God even existed, it's an example of God and His grace and mercy, and how long He extended His grace and mercy every day and way past what I deserved. Because God had a plan for me, He continued to answer my prayers, my thoughts, and my needs. All of what Xavier is was by God and His grace and mercy. Xavier is a gift from God, a shining star, a light to show us where God wants us to go. If you need an example, you need look no further than Xavier being put in a drug study where fifty percent of the participants would get the actual study drug and the other fifty percent would get a placebo drug. Xavier was selected to receive the study drug, and this drug was for his seizure condition that came on the scene in our lives. I am convinced to this day, and I give thanks to God daily, for hearing and answering our prayers. There have been so many more situations and instances such as this, and it aided us in understanding and navigating the spectrum, which helped us with decisions like speech therapy.

Even though Xavier was non-verbal, speech therapy was still important as far as bridging the communication gap. You see, even though he was non-verbal, the speech therapy helped Xavier to understand words, even though he could not speak. He would eventually develop one-word sentences to speak, and he could understand a whole sentence spoken by someone else. I think some parents of non-verbal children sometimes feel that speech therapy is a waste of time, and they don't put it high on the list of priorities when, in fact, it should be at the top. This is because what they understand is as important as how we understand their communication tools. One of Xavier's best assets is his great memory, which makes his ability to recall and associate a powerful tool in his learning. This is one of the reasons he was able to learn how to write his name with a pen or a pencil. His memory was the reason he could type and realize on his own when he misspelled a word; he would immediately backspace and correct it on his own. Xavier's teachers who recognized this, and the teachers that paid attention to the IEP meetings, understood this, and those are the teachers that had the most success with him academically and socially.

Xavier has such a calm demeanor now. Earlier in his life, shortly after the PDD (Pervasive Developmental Disorder) diagnosis, we learned how important occupational therapy was. It helped with Xavier's behavior, and by continuing with the occupational therapy, his behavior became calmer. Going to movies and going to restaurants was not an issue for him. He sits through movies even if they are not cartoons (Xavier loves the movie The Nutty Professor starring Eddie Murphy). The message I am sending here is: patience is vital in this journey. The results are coming; you just have to be willing to be disciplined enough to see it through. And this is why believing in a higher power is so important—having that unshakeable faith, that unbeatable faith, in something that is greater than yourself, greater than you. And for me, it is and always will be the God that I serve.

Chapter 4

Xploring and redefining

One of my favorite quotes, one that has resonated with me since I first read it in 1996, is from the prophet Kahlil Gibran: "Our children are not our own. They are but gifts that we give to the world." This quote aided my perception of how special Xavier really is. It helps me see him as I am supposed to see him, all the while seeing the power of God and all of God's power and God's strength, and further evidence of His presence not just in my life, but also in this world.

Even though some may have doubts because they are where I was a long time ago, confusing the will of man with the will of God, and giving credit or blame to God for all of the bad things and situations that happen in this world, in all actuality, it is the will of man. Wars are the will of man, violence the will of man, hatred the will of man, racism the will of man, genocide the will of man. Anything that has to do with bad is not of God. Free will is the one thing that God will not interfere with. God wants us to come to Him and submit to His will of our own volition, because in the will of God there is no suffering, there is no hatred, there are no wars, there is no racism, there is no selfishness. None of the things that clutter and cause difficulty to society are found in the will of God.

Seeing my son Xavier in this light and in this perspective does two things for me. One is it keeps me in awe of God and His power and His mercy, and makes me cherish this miracle, this blessing, that sees me as his father. I sometimes forget who God is, but Xavier will remind me. Xavier will show me what it is that I should see in God, because Xavier sees it in me. And no, I by no stretch of the imagination think that I am God or a god. What I am saying is that Xavier has shown me how I am supposed to be with my worship, how I am supposed to be with my faith and my prayers, and above all, the unshakeable belief in what it is my Heavenly Father is capable of and who He is.

My son has taught me that without having the advantage of speech. Xavier teaches me so much without saying anything, through a language that is only understood between he and I. It was once stated by a couple of people who watched the interaction between Xavier for just a brief moment, and they would come to the conclusion and say, "Y'all have your own language." And whenever this statement was made, I quickly realized that they had just witnessed the beauty of the relationship that existed between Xavier and I. It put smiles on people's faces, affirming my belief that God has sent him to me, God made him just for me, God chose me and this situation. Staying in the will of God will keep Xavier and I, and it will give Team Xavier everything we need to give Xavier the best quality of life.

Because everything Xavier gets from his birth mother is an important part of his growth and success. Everything his siblings do for him is vital to his quality of life and his ability to establish and develop relationships with people who are not his immediate family. Xavier's two sisters, his godmother, and my wife, who is not his birth mother but has loved him as her own, and the neighbor whose house Xavier would seek refuge in—all of this made up the village that poured into this miracle we call Xavier Duran Hutchins, also known as "The Big Dirty," "Big," "Zay," and my personal favorite, the name I call him when it's just Xavier and I, "Stinkem."

We all play a part in his development; we share his success; we all share the milestones. Because all of the ingredients for Xavier's success, I don't possess by myself. He needs everything that he gets from the other people in his life who love him and care about him. And so, having said that, I can honestly say that the gift we have given to the world is beautiful. It is an inspiring gift; it is a gift of love, a gift that keeps on giving, keeps on uplifting, and above all, the gift of HOPE that is wrapped up in this riddle, that is wrapped up in a rhyme, that is wrapped up in an enigma. We call him Xavier, and we color him love, which makes him universal, which makes him a gift to this world sent by my Lord and Savior, my Father, my God, to whom I am grateful, to whom I will praise and give thanks daily for His divine wisdom, for His grace and His mercy, for His patience—none of which I deserve, but it will never stop me from being grateful. And with this inspiration came the HOPE 4 Xavier FOUNDATION and the Xavier JOURNEY PODCAST, and all this came from our efforts to give Xavier the life he deserves.

Because every time someone sees him for the first time, they comment how happy Xavier looks. And it became my belief, and it became our effort, that every child on the spectrum should have what Xavier has. Every child on the spectrum should be as happy as Xavier. So, out of this belief, the HOPE 4 Xavier FOUNDATION was born, or birthed, whichever one you prefer. The fact that it came seven years later after the DREAM OUT LOUD 2000 non-profit, in retrospect, is not hard to explain but crazy to explain. It can all be linked to the feeling that I've had as long as I can remember: the feeling of helping people, the need or urge to help someone get to a better place in life and to provide a way or an avenue for them to get to where they wanted to. Seeing them do better, seeing them succeed, gave me and still gives me this feeling that is hard to explain, so I don't expect people to understand it. However, to those of us who know this unexplainable feeling and have and continue to have this feeling, you understand.

So, the birth of DREAM OUT LOUD 2000 came from my coaching at the local YMCA. What I discovered was that even after the basketball season was over, some of the young men would still come by the house to visit and talk about school, girls, and their future. In the conversation, I found out that a great many of them did not have the kind of relationship with their parents or guardian that they needed. And me, being the natural-born social worker that I am, I tried to be what was missing, and I was of the mindset that I could help them. The group of young men that I coached were from age ten to twelve, and I would move up with them until they became involved in high school sports.

But even then, they were still coming by to talk to me about life, and I used those moments to teach some life lessons. A lot of the drive and energy was drawn from the fact that I still, to this day, miss my dad, Samuel Lamar Hutchins. Losing him as early as I did in life has forever affected my temperament and perspective. As I got older, that bothered me more. The more I experienced life, the more I found myself silently asking, "What would be different if my father was here?" I asked myself this often, and this feeling at times would make me sad, make me withdraw, and really dampen my thought process, not to mention my spirit.

When I spoke to some of those young men, I wanted to protect them. They trusted me, and I'll even go as far as to say they cared about me too. Like my son Xavier, trust was the binding tie that bound us. Even to this day, some of the young men are in their thirties, and when they see me and Xavier, it is always a small love fest. They greet Xavier and marvel at his size, and then tell me how much they appreciated what I did for them by talking to them, showing them love, and giving them guidance.

One night, Xavier and I were up watching TV; we were watching a Ma and Pa Kettle marathon. It was around eleven-thirty at night when the doorbell rang. So, I got up and looked out the peephole in the door, and to my surprise, I saw about eight sixteen-year-old young men on my porch. I opened the door, and one of the young men said, "Coach, we saw your light on, so we decided to stop by." I was both amused and puzzled, but I told them to come in. We sat and talked for the better part of an hour, and then they got up to leave. They all "dapped me up," as they call it. They all asked Xavier to give them five, and he did.

A couple of days later, I saw one of the young men's mothers, and I told her about them coming by, what time it was, and how long they stayed. I voiced my concern about them being out that late at night, and the young lady hit me with a revelation when she said, "We all should be thankful that they were at your house. They could have been out doing something wrong and getting in trouble, but they came and sat with you." She said, "And for that, I am grateful that they have you." It was like an epiphany, and I said, "You know what, you are right."

So, DREAM OUT LOUD 2000 became an outlet, a mentoring resource, a place where the young men could come and talk about not just problems, but dreams as well, be it college, trade schools, careers, life choices. I believe to this day that it is my relationship with my son Xavier that allowed them to trust in me and to trust me with their feelings and their dreams, and in some cases, some very delicate situations. I never broke that trust, and in return, they had a sense of not wanting to let me down, and I certainly did not want to let them down. I love and respect each and every one of those relationships because as much as they come back and tell me what I did for them, they did just as much for me.

So, DREAM OUT LOUD and its meaning: "DREAM" was something that I was realizing when I would ask a ten-year-old what they wanted to be when they grew up, and too many times there was silence. Not like when I was growing up, that question would be answered quickly with "a policeman," "a fireman," or "a race car driver," or in my case, a superhero (Batman and Superman were my heroes of choice). But now, when I asked that question, I was getting the shoulder shrug way too often, and that became my entry into their imagination: to get them to DREAM again and to say that DREAM out loud. The "two thousand" has nothing to do with the year; the "two thousand" was the number of lives that I want to change for the better before I leave this earth. Hence, the organization DREAM OUT LOUD 2000, which was launched in the summer of 2008. I took the basketball program from the YMCA and turned it into an AAU basketball program, and I had about thirty young men throughout the summer which kept them busy and out of trouble. More importantly, it taught them to dream, and some of them got on the radar of college recruiters, getting a chance to play college ball—mostly at small schools, nothing major. Occasionally, I would also have a girls' team, so now we're talking about thirty boys and twelve girls.

Mind you, this was the year 2008. The housing market had crashed, I had lost my job, and I lost my house. I depleted my 401k trying to hold on to my house, and I was getting three hundred and seventy-six dollars a week. I was paying for uniforms and paying tournament fees out of that three hundred and seventy-six dollars. So, on a weekend when I had to pay all three teams' tournament fees, that would total four hundred and fifty dollars. Donations were needed but not always available, so the young men would get buckets and beg in parking lots at grocery stores and stand at intersections and do the same. I got invitations in the mail all the time, and with my income being limited, I couldn't afford to go to every one of them. However, it meant so much to them; they would come to me and say, "Coach, we got the tournament fee. Can we play now?" To me, that was God making a way, and to me, it was God saying I was headed in the right direction, which was why we prayed the Lord's Prayer before and after every game.

Again, this was about trust, and my relationship with my son Xavier gives me the credibility. Because of the nature of Xavier and my relationship, the young men could see the magic and the beauty of this relationship. If you have the ability to see how special it is, then you can see God and His power on full display. Just as Xavier changed my life for the better, the relationship between those young men and (occasionally) the young ladies did the same for me and them. We won a couple of championships and were runner-up in a few more. Some of the conversations between those young people and I (they are in their late twenties and early thirties now) are about those episodes, and they are recalled with an appreciation and an admiration that enhanced and enriched all of our lives—theirs and mine.

It is interesting how times and events can prepare you for "what is next" in life, especially when you are not paying attention. The seven years prior to me starting my second non-profit were actually getting me ready to lead Team Xavier into what God had been preparing me for all my life: the DREAM OUT LOUD 2000 mentoring organization was and still is something near and dear to my heart. The passion and purpose that I wasn't aware of until later were responsible for some great feelings, some great memories, and yes, there was some crying, some frustration, some disappointment, and there was some redemption and rebirth. All of this is a byproduct of being a human being. All of these things are part of the human experience, and it is something that makes us, and in some cases breaks us. However, the great thing about the human experience is that failure or redemption is always possible, depending on what you, as a human being, want to do. Because when I have the heart-to-heart talk with young people, then and now, it's that your life has two stories to be told: one is the one that the world will tell, and the one that you write. In both instances, you are in control over which one the world will hear, and that will depend a great deal on how much you love yourself and how much you care about the people who love you, the people who spend a part of their lives loving you, uplifting and upholding you because they see your worth, sometimes before you, and sometimes more importantly, they see your worth when you don't.

So the years are passing, and we at Team Xavier are gaining knowledge and having life experiences that, on the outside looking in, you would never know. It's not that we were hiding anything; it was how well we were handling it. The affirmation for us came from the smile and laughter that came from Xavier, and from a community standpoint, Xavier became a standard that people looked at and were put at ease. This was because we went to movies, we went on vacations, he got haircuts with no incident, crowds did not bother him, changing from one activity was a smooth transition, again, without incident. And so, more phone calls started happening, more conversations in the grocery stores and the Walmarts, and people would ask, "How did you get him to always be so calm and happy? He listens, and you all don't seem to have to repeat yourself. How did you all get him to this point?"

Two things were taking place at the same time, again, while we were not looking, and more so, even I wasn't paying attention. One of the things that was happening was that people were really paying attention to Xavier whenever he was out in public, whether we were out as a family or Xavier just being out with his birth mom or just Xavier and I. The one constant, the one thing they always commented on, was how happy and how calm he was. And people wanted to know what they called the "secret" or the "key" to Xavier and his success. So, Xavier became a symbol of what autism is, what autism could be, and most of all, he was a symbol of HOPE. For some people, just getting that diagnosis, hope is a very important component when it comes to "what next?" "How do I do this?" Seeing Xavier inspires this in people because the landscape and the understanding of autism are so different now than what they were in 1994 when Xavier was first diagnosed. Case in point, in 1994, after Xavier was diagnosed, I started purchasing books, magazines, watching movies, looking at documentaries, and I had a t-shirt that read, "ONE IN EVERY EIGHTY-EIGHT CHILDREN WILL BE BORN WITH AUTISM. ONE OF THEM WAS MINE." Four years later, that was old data. It had gone from one in every eighty-eight to one in every sixty-four. And the thing that I quickly noticed was that it was trending in the wrong direction, and that the trend was rapidly going in a negative direction.

I was simply not satisfied with the limited attention and apparent lack of new research. I was reading and searching the web every day, and what I found wasn't new; it was basically the same information presented differently. We were of the mindset that more attention needed to be brought to this neurological disorder. I just felt like more, or at least enough, wasn't being done.

Then one day, Xavier and I were in a local supermarket. We could hear a child screaming a couple of aisles over, and I could hear the child's mother trying to calm him down. As I listened, I recognized the voice; it was the voice of my former neighbor, Wanda Lene Emerson Thompson. We grew up living right next door to each other, not more than six hundred feet apart. We rode the same bus, we played at each other's house, and her brother and my brother were best friends. Wanda even dated my brother for a while, so we were like family. At this point, I hadn't seen her in what must have been ten years.

So, Xavier and I went over to see if we could be of some assistance. As I asked her what was going on, she informed me that her son had autism and that she heard my son had autism as well. I said yes, he does. She then started to ask the questions that people had begun asking us: "How did we get him so calm, and he seems so happy?" Of course, I told her about the importance of early intervention and the support system, ABA therapy, and speech therapy. I also informed her about the Marcus Center for official diagnosis. I told her that if she had any questions, I would be glad to help her, and if I didn't have the answer, I would be happy to help her find them.

Now, Wanda is one of the sweetest people anyone will ever meet. She is a giver, always willing and looking to help anyone she can. She had this calm demeanor about her and a very strong belief in the higher power she served, the same higher power I serve, that power being God Almighty. The conversation went on for a while, and she continued to ask questions, and I answered them as best I could with the life experience I had and with the information I had gained from reading articles, books, and watching documentaries and movies. Wanda then said, "You know, you have a lot of information. We should start an organization to help get this information to people." I thought that would be a great idea; however, I had no idea how or where to get started.

So, Xavier and I went home, and I got on the internet and came up with information on for-profit and non-profit organizations. I went with a non-profit because I was under the impression that DREAM OUT LOUD 2000 was completely different from the HOPE 4 Xavier FOUNDATION. As it turns out, it was not. Now, bear in mind, I didn't have a job; I was getting unemployment: three hundred and seventy-six dollars a week. To start a non-profit from zero is around fifteen hundred dollars, of which I had none. So, my brother helped me get the EIN number and register with the state of Georgia. With my funds being very limited, it was a slow process, and I had to put it in park for a minute.

Fast forward three years later, Wanda was in the hospital from complications of lupus, and unfortunately, she was dying. However, she was still holding on to her faith that God would and could heal her if it be God's will. My brother was visiting her occasionally in the hospital, and one Saturday my brother called, and I asked him how she was. He informed me that medically there was nothing that could be done, and it was all in God's hands. My brother said she asked him if I had got that organization started yet, and my brother informed her that I had hit a brick wall and that I was still gathering resources to start it. My brother says she told him that when she gets out of this hospital, "Tell Sam that I am going to help him start that organization." And ladies and gentlemen, three days later, she passed.

I kept replaying my brother's conversation with her that he had shared with me. Wanda had such faith in God, and she kept that faith until she transitioned. So, when 2015 came and we launched, the HOPE 4 Xavier FOUNDATION was born. To honor Wanda's legacy, to honor her memory and her spirit, we established the WANDA LENE EMERSON THOMPSON MEMORIAL SCHOLARSHIP AWARD so that her spirit will live on, her caring nature will not be forgotten, and it would help drive us and reinforce our passion and our purpose to bring "AWARENESS AND EMPOWERMENT WHILE EMPOWERING." This became our charge; this became our assignment, and we carry it to this day. We carry it with pride, we carry it with love.

The scholarship consists of five hundred dollars cash, a brand new laptop, a plaque commemorating the recipient as the Wanda Lene Emerson Thompson Memorial Award, and a four-year partnership with the recipient, which means that if you need money for anything like books or equipment, we would be a resource while they are in school. All of this is done at a black-tie gala, which is our biggest fundraiser. It not only funds the scholarship but also pays for the literature that we pass out at trade shows and speaking engagements and pamphlets that we leave in churches wherever the churches display their literature. It's free; however, the cost to reproduce the literature is not free, nor are the T-shirts that we sell. While donations have become a part of our mission, it's not consistent enough that we can stop the fundraising efforts.

The face of this and the driving force behind this, the passion that fuels the efforts which is essential to the purpose, is my son Xavier Duran Hutchins, also known as "The Big Dirty," "Big," "Zay," and "Stinkem." The miracle, the blessing, the gift from God showing us the way, inspiring us to never give up. Xavier is great at taking away confusion and complications with that grin that turns into a smile that removes any doubt or any worry or anything that you conceived as a problem. That smile of his has the ability to make you believe that everything is going to be better, and if it gets better, then it being alright is just around the corner. Yes indeed, HOPE is what Xavier brings into the lives of the people that he comes in contact with. Hope is all around him, and it's the message he wants Team Xavier to convey. And it is that message of hope that we bring because what Xavier has taught me personally is that this message that we are conveying, this message that Xavier is inspiring, is bigger than us because we are showing people what's possible. We are showing people that given an opportunity, the possibilities are endless, and all of this is because of the God who sent Xavier to us because, "OUR CHILDREN ARE NOT OUR OWN; THEY ARE BUT GIFTS WE GIVE TO THE WORLD." Does this sound familiar?

Describes Xavier's sensory sensitivities, including sound, light, touch, taste and smell. The impact on daily life and strategies employed to manage these sensitivities. Illustrates the importance of creating a calming environment.

Xavier At the Atlanta Haws Game Verses the Lakers

It was universally believed that all autistic kids or adults don't like change, and that it causes a real disruption in their day because routine is so critical to maintain. To a certain degree, this is true. However, with Xavier, what we found out—and what some people probably missed—is how important the element of trust is. We came to this conclusion, or discovery, by chance, and it became a milestone moment for us and a very integral part of Xavier and his education and his development of relationships with people.

These two parts of his life would serve as the basis for the foundation of his growth in this world, and it all happened one night when Xavier and I attended a professional basketball game. Now, bear in mind that Xavier has zero interest in any sport of any kind, yet he would watch an entire sporting event with me and never pay attention to the game itself. But he was paying attention to me, and he would imitate every move I made and repeat every sound I made. So, when I said, "YES," he would repeat it. If I said, "Shoot," he would say "shoot" (I do not use profanity). And if I raised both arms in a triumphant gesture, he would do the same. All this was building up and leading to the one thing that most people miss when it comes to caring for someone on the spectrum, and that element is TRUST.

This was why our relationship is so special, because it became very apparent that he trusts me more than anyone in the world. It is the reason I can get him to come from under the bed when no one else could. It is the reason that he would go places with me that he would not go with anyone else, and it is all based on the element of trust and the level of that trust. There were things that you normally would not pay attention to, like he would only ride in the front seat of my car and no one else. It went unnoticed until some conversations were had and some actions were observed. Again, all of this came into existence one night at an Atlanta Hawks basketball game.

Now, I'll put this in context so that you will understand the complexity of this soon-to-be milestone moment. The Atlanta Hawks were playing the Los Angeles Lakers. I am a huge Lakers fan, and I have been since 1975 when the Milwaukee Bucks traded Kareem Abdul-Jabbar to the Lakers. Since we live in Georgia, I only get to see them once a year in person. This was the second year of the championship run for Shaquille O'Neal and Kobe Bryant, and again, we are talking about an arena that holds over 20,000 people, and the place had more Lakers fans in attendance than Atlanta Hawks fans.

If we consider the common belief that autistic children don't like crowds, Xavier was truly dispelling that myth. As we walked through the arena, he was holding my hand, as we always do, and he was so relaxed. He watched people as we strolled throughout the crowd, waving at all the pretty girls with his free hand and saying "hey." Some of them responded, and some did not. To the ones that spoke back to him, he would give off this little giggle, and he even got a few compliments as some of the ladies called him handsome.

We stopped by the concession stand to get him his Skittles and popcorn and then made our way to our seats. It was halfway through the first quarter when we finally settled in. It was noisy, and the game was kind of close. Then, on this particular play, Shaq O'Neal went up for one of his monster dunks, and the place erupted. For the first time that evening, Xavier was afraid. He leaned over, grabbed me, and I could feel his heart beating. As I hugged him and rubbed his head, I whispered in his ear, "I got you. I got you." I could feel his heartbeat slowing down, and he was becoming calmer. Then he looked at me, and I was smiling at him, and then he smiled back. For the rest of the game, when the place erupted in response to a great play, he would look at me, and I would say, "I got you," and he calmly watched the rest of the game without any incident.

However, there was someone sitting in front of us, and when Xavier jumped, he accidentally kicked the back of their seat. It upset him, and rightfully so. I apologized and offered to buy him a coke or a beer, and he refused, which was his choice. The rest of the game and the night were fun for us both, and it served as a milestone moment for Team Xavier. I shared the story with his mom when we returned, and this was particularly useful as he was just one year into his seizure condition. Because when he would have a seizure, we would hold him until he came out of it, and again, whispering in his ear that simple phrase, "I got you," it always calmed him down and brought him back to his happy place. Loud noises never bothered him, and large crowds do not faze him as long as he can see my face, and my smile seems to build trust and give him peace of mind.

So we attend baseball games at what was then Turner Field where the Atlanta Braves play, the Georgia Dome, home of the Atlanta Falcons. He would go with me without hesitation, and he is not a sports fan; he just wanted to be around me. Because in Xavier's eyes, I could fix anything. In Xavier's eyes, no harm would ever come to him. Xavier believed that, and whatever he wanted, if he let me know he wanted it, Xavier knew that he would get it. Xavier believes that I have endless resources and that nothing will be denied. Does this sound like something that the Bible teaches us about God? How nothing is impossible with God? We can rest assured that God will protect us, and for those of us who have faith in who and what God can do, and when you believe that and you practice this, then you come to the conclusion that Xavier has when it comes to me.

By him having this kind of trust in me, by Xavier having this kind of trust, this kind of belief in me, it gave me the blueprint as to how I am supposed to be when it comes to the God that I serve. I learned this from this incredible human being that I call my son, and for someone who is non-verbal, my son speaks volumes. This is my testimony: Xavier saved my soul. Xavier got me back in touch and on the path that God had been preparing me for all my life. My son loves me like I am supposed to love God. My son trusts me like I am supposed to trust God. Xavier believes in me like I am supposed to believe in God. Xavier taught me this without verbally speaking a word, and through this amazing human being, this earth angel, this miracle that I get to love and witness every day, he showed me the way.

This experience has taught me about God's grace and God's mercy, God's patience, God's tolerance, and it taught me and is still teaching me that God has a purpose and a plan for everyone. God never fails, and God protects us as long as we stay in the will of God. No one has ever gotten lost following God, and God is the master at taking something that was meant for bad and turning it into something good and using it to uplift God's righteous and holy name. I ask for forgiveness for all my years of ignorance. I have to ask for forgiveness for my defiance, and I have to say thank you, God. Thank you, Xavier, for saving a wretch like me. As the song says, "He thought I was worth saving," and I have my son Xavier combined with the goodness of God. So, on that day that I pass from this life to the next, when I have gone my last mile, as the song says, when I take my rest and I am welcomed into heaven, I will be able to say to my Lord and Savior, thank you, and if heaven is my home (and I believe it will be), it will be because I was shown the way to my purpose by God through my son, Xavier Duran Hutchins.

Chapter 5

Xceeding the unknown

After years of gaining experience and knowledge, most of it being lived experience and some obtained from reading and research, along with some from movies and TV shows like "The Good Doctor"—which, by the way, started out very good and then did what Hollywood does, leaning heavily on entertainment and less on education, at which point they lost me. However, there were some educational points for me that, upon doing my research, I found were spot on with the information, but I digress.

I learned that at the core of what Xavier was, the thing that helped him help himself, and if you paid attention, it helped you help him as well, was understanding how important logic and trust are with him. Because these are Xavier, and once these two pillars are what his understanding is, then you are on your way to having a better relationship with Xavier. What I learned, more so than most of us on Team Xavier, was how he moved, why he moved the way he did, and I firmly believe that this is why his temperament was that of a gentle soul and why he was so easygoing. Because the third pillar of what gives him a leg up on people was his uncanny ability to read people.

Now, I am going to go back a little and speak on his logic pillar. This was a topic of discussion at a couple of his IEP meetings because, for whatever reason, when he was going from one grade to the next and when a new teacher was involved, somehow the new teacher would not read the notes from the previous IEP meetings from the past school year. So, we had to repeat the premise of explaining Xavier and his logic. Let me explain here what is meant and what I mean when I speak of Xavier's logic. It is really no different from common sense. If Xavier comes across a situation that is new to him and he doesn't understand it, he will look at the people around him, and if Xavier sees or senses apprehension on the face or in the spirit of anyone around him, then Xavier is not going to be a willing participant.

Because he doesn't see or sense the level of trust that Xavier himself deems necessary, then it's not going to happen. At six-foot-four and three hundred forty-eight pounds, not too many people can make him. That's what Xavier has with me: if I'm in the room, he'll seek out my face, and in particular, my eyes. If he sees me smiling and if he sees me unshaken, his trust kicks in, and he will participate and allow whatever is going on to continue.

A case in point happened one weekend. He discovered that jumping on the bed, while fun, can lead to getting hurt if you're not careful. In this instance, he split his lip and required a few stitches. So, Xavier had to be taken to the emergency room for said stitches. I had to meet them at the hospital. Before I got there, they were trying to put an instrument on the tip of his finger to get one of his vital signs. Because it had a red light on it, Xavier thought it was hot. A couple of years back, he had burned his hand on the stove, and he remembered that the eye on the stove was red when he burned his hand. So, naturally, when he saw red, it triggered this memory, and this is why he refused to let them place it on his finger (they even tried to hold his arms, to no avail). These were the types of things that only I paid attention to and would remember.

When I got there, I asked him how he was and gave him a nose kiss. The doctor remarked that the nurse couldn't get his vital sign because he refused to let them place the monitor with the red light. So, I asked if I could see the instrument. I got Xavier's attention and told him to look, and I placed it on my finger. Of course, his mom and the doctor explained to me that they had tried that before I got there. What they didn't understand was that the element of trust, or the level of trust, that was in that room was not there until I got there, because that is what Xavier has for me more than any human being in this world. So, I placed it on my finger and I said, "Look." Xavier looked at me, and I showed him that it was okay. As I took it off, he stuck out his finger, and

I placed it on his finger. The doctor looked at me, then he looked at Xavier's mom, and the doctor then asked me, "Where were you forty-five minutes ago?" This again demonstrated Xavier's logic: his logic has to have an element of trust, and again, he trusts no one.

More than me even, when riding in a car, Xavier will not ride in the front seat of his mother's car, even when it's just the two of them. I think on occasion he will with his oldest sister, but with his mother, he heads straight for the backseat and buckles up. Now, with me, it is always the front seat, no matter who or how many people are going; he is riding in the front seat with me. That is the bond that he and I have.

Xavier believes in me like nobody else does. Xavier believes that there is nothing that I, as his father, cannot do. Does this sound familiar? My son was teaching me how I am supposed to see the God that I serve. I am supposed to have that kind of faith; I am supposed to have that level of trust in my God. Xavier taught me this, and this revelation carries me to this day. Xavier taught me this without saying a word. He is the reason that I gained the ability to listen with my heart, and once I learned this, I could hear him better, and I could hear God better, which laid the foundation for what has turned out to be the most life-changing experiences and life-changing relationships that I have. And I thank God for him.

God is the best at taking something that was meant to be bad, something that was meant to be used for evil, and not only making it turn out good, but it will also be used for God and His glory. So, if you get to heaven and you see me, it will be because of my son, my best friend, my miracle, my blessing sent to me by God. You see, this is proof that God will meet you where you are in your situation, even if you are not going down or traveling the path that God had for you.

Xavier, his birth, our relationship, is all heaven-sent, all in God's plan. And the plan was to get me back into the will of God, and I am thankful. I am blessed way past what I deserved; however, it will not stop me from being grateful, and I am so very grateful. It has become part of who I am: to tell this story about the glory of a father and his son, and how his love for his son carries and uplifts not just Xavier and I, but all who come in contact with us. All who come into contact with us, as our story has become the face of autism in our community. Xavier is the actual tour guide; I am just his assistant or his interpreter. And through him and with him, we are changing not the whole world, just the part we live in.

Chapter 6

Xtream not so much

Early on, we had to deal with a lot of preconceived notions, not only about Xavier's diagnosis but also people's ideas and lack of understanding about what autism truly was and all it entails. They didn't grasp the whole concept of the autism spectrum and what it included, nor did they understand that everyone on the spectrum isn't the same, and that having autism isn't a "one size fits all" diagnosis. Every diagnosis is different and as unique as the individual whom it affects, and there's no cookie-cutter procedure that works on every person on the spectrum in the same way. For example, what works in the development of one person on the spectrum may have the reverse effect on another. It really depends on where the individual is on the spectrum, and knowing where an individual is on the spectrum by everyone involved with them is detrimental to their success.

Seeing how they process information and understanding their degree of comprehension is crucial to the amount of success that will come. That's why you'll hear stories of amazing accomplishment, and their backstory is almost always one of perseverance and determination, with a team behind them that wanted nothing more than to give the individual, their loved one, the opportunity to have and live the best quality of life with the fewest amount of boundaries and barriers that society will try to place on them. When it came to Xavier, we understood this early on.

Some of the obstacles that we faced with Xavier had nothing to do with him having autism; it was his imposing size. As a six-year-old, Xavier was nearly five feet tall and close to one hundred pounds. However, he was so easygoing and had such a gentle nature, and harming someone wasn't on his mind. Because he was so much bigger than his classmates, some of the kids were afraid of him, which is why I used the word "imposing" to describe his presence from the perspective of the classmate who viewed him as intimidating. So, there were a lot of unscheduled parent meetings with other parents to make sure they understood and to ease their minds about Xavier and his gentle nature, and assure them that he had no intention to hurt, harm, or endanger anyone. This is why we described him as "The Gentle Giant," because that's exactly who and what he was.

In the summer of 1999, Xavier developed a seizure condition that, in addition to the autism, now required him to take a total of twenty-five pills a day for his seizure condition: fifteen in the morning and ten at night. Now, mind you, this didn't stop the seizures; it helped control them, and once it was under control, they subsided substantially. He went from four to five a day to one to two a day, with the occasional uptick when he caught a cold or when spring came around. Of course, as he got older and grew in size, the dosage had to be adjusted, and it got to a point where the seizure medication was losing its effectiveness, and we were really up against it as a family.

Then, on one of his three-month visits to the neurologist, it was mentioned to us that a new study drug was in the testing stages, and they didn't know how long it would be before it went before the FDA for approval. However, if we decided to participate in the study, there was a fifty-fifty chance that he would receive the study drug, because only half who entered the study would get the study drug and the other half would get the placebo drug, and there was no guarantee that my son would receive the drug. However, as long as we were participating in the study, all of Xavier's medicines and doctor visits would be free, and there was a gas stipend because we actually lived almost sixty miles away. So, we really had nothing to lose; even if he didn't get the study drug, the other benefits were advantageous for Xavier and us as a family.

After about two weeks in the study, Xavier experienced a downward trend in his seizure frequency, which made it very evident that he was in the half that was receiving the study drug.

This was evident to me that God was working in our favor and giving us everything we needed. God was providing, and it was at this point I was on my journey to renewing my faith in the God that I now serve. I now had to reconsider the possibility that yes, there was and is a higher power. This event was step one, and as you keep reading, you will read and witness another moment of faith from my perspective. Xavier and Team Xavier were back on track and on our way.

Chapter 7

Xpectations put in order

Xavier's journey was a journey that was filled with several milestones and breakthroughs, some good, some bad, some ups, some downs. Along the way, there were some amazing teachers and paraprofessionals that had the temperament and the kindness that it took to help formulate my son's educational experience. They looked within themselves and found the way to meet my son where he was. They recognized his strengths, and those special ones were the ones who would not deny my son the opportunity, judged by a preconceived notion about the perception that all autistic people have built-in limitations, when in a lot of cases, the limitation is only in your head and usually based on limited knowledge that you've heard or some movie you've seen. So, I salute Mr. Jimmy Houston, Miss Jill Green, Mrs. Ursula Woods, and a couple more whose names escape me at the moment of this writing. And also to the principal at Winder-Barrow High School, Mr. Al Darby. He put forth a special effort to help make my son's high school experience the best that he could, and he was personally involved. I will never forget that on graduation night, he made arrangements for my son and I to receive his "diploma" first, because he took into consideration that Xavier may get restless and he may want to leave after an hour, because the ceremony was over two hours long. So when the graduates were called, his name was called first, and he and I walked across the stage, got his diploma, and went back to our seat. I waited for him to give me the sign to leave, and to our surprise, he stayed through the entire ceremony. It was almost like he knew that this was a special moment for Team Xavier and he wanted to take it all in.

Xavier was becoming somewhat of a local celebrity as he went from elementary to high school. The eyes of the community were a lot more on autism because of my son. He had become the face for autism in our community, and with the emergence of his seizure condition along with autism, his day-to-day plight was of interest to everyone in the community to some degree on several levels because they saw how happy he was. He always seemed to be in a happy state of mind, and it was the one thing that we constantly heard, and it was that he always seemed to be so happy. That small statement empowered us so much, and it helped lead to the formation of my non-profit, inspired by his journey with autism and the message that his life was sending to the world. I would get questions like, "How do you get him to sit still for a haircut?" or "Why doesn't change upset him?" or "Do you guys have trouble shopping with him?" or "How is the experience of going out to eat?" And this would turn out to be one of the pillars that we would use to build the spiritual foundations for the Hope 4 Xavier Foundation, and the main thing that I would tell any parent or caregiver was the importance of early intervention. Xavier was diagnosed at two with PDD, which two years later would be called autism, because early on we got him.

We had to leave movie theaters, we had to leave restaurants, but we stayed with his physical therapy, we stayed with his ABA, we stayed with his speech therapy. Early on, it was frustrating because we were seeing very little progress from ages two to five years old, and we started questioning if we were taking the right course of action to give our son the best opportunity for the best quality of life. So we made the decision to stay the course. The program that got us started was introduced to us by a lady named Miss Ellen Day, and the program was called Baby's Can't Wait. At the age of two, I can't imagine what his quality of life would have been had we waited until he was ten or twelve. And don't get me wrong, it's never too late, even at those older ages, but what I will say is that your task for the best quality of life is still possible and obtainable; it's just significantly harder and maybe even difficult, but not impossible.

It has been my experience personally, and after hearing from other parents, that around age eight is when you get introduced to drugs like Ritalin and Adderall, none of which I view as medication that helps the child/adult. It's more for the teacher to help them maintain the child so that they don't disrupt the class, because I have always heard that there is a zombie effect, and it was something that we would not agree to. They kept presenting that option to us until his sophomore year in high school, and then they got the message that it wasn't an option that we would consider. Why, do you ask? Because, don't forget, my son is nonverbal, so he couldn't say "this makes me feel funny," "this makes my head hurt," or "this makes me see blue mules." So, the language barrier was something that I constantly had to remind doctors and teachers, as it would seem as though they would forget, which brings me back to my point about the importance of early intervention.

And when it comes to IEP meetings, there should be a team concept to it, and there are three entities that are involved but not always present. The components are: first and foremost is the child, and the focus should never go away from the fact that the child is first, but also the child is the most important part of this whole equation. Then there is, of course, the family, whatever that consists of, because that dynamic could be a single parent, male or female, or it could consist of a grandparent that is taking care of a child, or a child could be in a same-sex situation—could be two women, could be two men, it doesn't matter in this regard, because as I stated earlier, the child is the most important component in this equation. So, as long as whoever is in this position, you still need to know and understand and concentrate all your efforts into doing what's best for the child. And of course, the third component is the educational system. All three should be in unison with whatever the goal is, to make sure that the efforts are geared toward one goal, and that goal is what's best for the child, and you all become a team and making sure that the learning experience is a good, if not great, experience. No matter how frustrating or impossible it may seem, you have to have the mindset that if not this way, let's find another way, because there is always another way. Your faith will show you, your faith will guide you. God never fails, and your faith and prayers are your connection to God who is able and will never fail.

Chapter 8

Xpectancy anything is possible

It was the year 2000. The internet was still in its early stages, and technology was moving very fast. Home computers and access to the internet, and the ability to maneuver and surf the web, were "the thing." There was dial-up, there was WebTV, then came cable, then there were internet providers like AOL, EarthLink, PeoplePC, NetZero, to name a few. I was not too invested in it; I only had WebTV. It was entertaining, not to the degree it is now; I mean, you couldn't subscribe to premium channels, and you couldn't download music—not yet, but it wasn't that far off.

Then one day, a friend of mine was purchasing his children a new desktop computer and was giving away the old one. He asked me if I was interested in it, and I said, "Sure, how much do you want for it?" He said, "You can have it; you will just need to get a printer." So I said, "Okay, thanks," not realizing what was about to take place would be one of the great milestones in my life. So I took it home, set it up, plugged the cord into the modem, and just like that, we were on the internet. My son Xavier and his sister were there watching and waiting with anticipation, and when I finished, my daughter, with Xavier sitting right beside her, started surfing the web. So I removed myself from the moment as I realized my work there was done.

Over the course of the next two days, I brought home a printer; it was a color printer, nothing elaborate. And again, once I integrated the computer to the printer, my services were no longer needed. Over the course of approximately two weeks, I started to notice these printouts from the Notepad component of the computer, and it was cars being listed, which puzzled me because my daughter, who is five years older than Xavier, was now thirteen, and Xavier was eight, so they are five years apart. So I came to the conclusion that my daughter was dropping me not-so-subtle hints about cars and driving. I mean, I'm seeing the printouts and the cars listed are BMW, Acura, Lexus, Mercedes-Benz, Cadillac, Lincoln, and I was thinking, "Yes, this is my daughter dropping hints," because at the time, I am driving a 1995 Thunderbird; I didn't see Ford or Chevy anywhere on the list.

And then one day, I saw a Notepad printout that had the names of the stores where we did the majority of our shopping. They were all in this plaza; we would just park the car and walk from store to store. There was Marshalls, TJ Maxx, Ross, Home Depot, and a movie theater called Colonial 18. Now this really has me puzzled, yet I still didn't ask any questions. I'm still of the assumption that it's my daughter. And then one day, I come home and I see a Notepad printout, and the color of the font is now written in red. So now, in my mind, I know this has to be my daughter. Mind you, at this time, I only used the web to read newspapers from different states because I'm a huge sports fan: Miami Dolphins and the LA Lakers. So my papers of choice were the Miami Herald and the LA Times.

So a couple of weeks go by, and I asked my daughter about the Notepad printouts. I asked her if she was trying to give me a hint, and she has a puzzled look on her face, and she asked, "Why do you ask that?" And I replied, "I've been seeing these Notepad printouts with the names of cars." And she said, "That's not me, that's Xavier printing those out, not me." And of course, I raised my eyebrow in disbelief, and my response was, "Yeah, right." And she insisted that it was indeed Xavier.

So as fate would have it, I got off work early one day, and as I came to the door, I was not greeted by my normal beeline from Xavier. So I walked through the house as I heard a sound coming from what had become the computer room. I knew it wasn't my daughter because it was not time for her to be home from school. And when I got close enough to see a figure in the room and recognized that it was Xavier, and he was in Notepad, and he was typing with two hands, head up, looking at the monitor, and in a row he had typed: ACURA, BMW, CADILLAC, MERCEDES-

BENZ, JAGUAR, HOME DEPOT, ROSS, T.J. MAXX, MARSHALLS, TARGET, and was in the process of spelling COLONIAL 18 CINEMA. And what made it even more amazing was that he didn't have anything to copy from; he didn't have anything to reference what he was spelling. He was doing all of this from memory. He was remembering what he had seen in the Sunday paper, and he had everything spelled correctly.

And yes, this was one of those moments, this was one of those milestones that maybe small to someone not familiar with what goes on raising a child on the spectrum. So it may be hard to see why every milestone is to be celebrated and appreciated, because we never know when the next one will come, or even if another milestone will come. So you embrace all the emotions that come with these achievements, and I was no different in this case. I went out and bought a new computer from our local Radio Shack. I bought a new color printer. I was so happy, as we all were. So when my daughter came home, I had to tell her that she was right, and of course, she said that she tried to tell me, and I told her I owed her something, and she said nothing. I think she could see the joy that was on my face, so much so I would not have minded if she had said, "I told you so," simply because she told me so.

Chapter 9

Not Xpecting the unimaginable

There is a quote that, when I first heard it, encapsulated so many of my thoughts about life. Things like, "How did this person get to the place they are in life today?" "What was their mental makeup, and how had life's sum total of that life guided them or misguided them to the place and position in life that they now find themselves in?" And "How much of the guiding or misguiding was a direct result of who they are and how they handled the situation or the experience that presented itself to that individual?"

So there were and are questions like, "Did I live to satisfy my spirit or did I live to satisfy my body?" And "What part of my makeup (body and soul) made the right decision? Was it my soul or was it my body? Did my soul make the choices that my body rejected and lead to a bad decision?" These kinds of questions, at least for me, were answered in this quote that I heard from one of my favorite TV shows called Spenser: For Hire. It was a quotation from a book that the main character would quote from quite often, and it is: "FOR OF THE SOUL THE BODY FORM DOTH TAKE FOR SOUL IS FORMED DOTH THE BODY MAKE." This was from a book called The Faerie Queene. However, when I looked up the original quote, it actually came from Aristotle, the Greek philosopher, which apparently was a topic of discussion way back then, before Edmund Spenser and his book, and certainly before Xavier was born.

And even though it is his imposing presence that I and everyone has always marveled at, simply because he has always been big for his age, which is also why one of his nicknames is "BIG," and yet while being so imposing physically, Xavier has such a sweet, calm, easygoing, peaceful nature about him. That infectious smile and that laughter—him being 6 foot 4, 348 pounds—always puts a smile on my face and a warm feeling around my heart. And it is almost like he has a superpower when it comes to discernment. Xavier's ability to know what a person is like, even if he was meeting them for the first time; it just seems like he can tell if they are a good person or not. His uncanny ability to read people's hearts along with a memory like an elephant is what he stands on, and in his defense, not that he needs defending, it has served him well because he has been right one hundred percent of the time.

And over the years, that bond that he and I have, that he and I hold, and the space in time where only he and I exist, I am taken to quite often. Sometimes I am taken there by a memory, and it still has that same effect, however, not to the degree it does when it is just Xavier and I. And I love it when just Xavier and I are riding in the car listening to one of his favorite songs (on repeat).

And he's dancing in the passenger seat, rocking back and forth. If he notices me lost in thought, my forehead wrinkled, and if I'm not smiling, he'll take that massive left hand and extend it as if to say, "Whatever you're thinking about that has taken the smile away from your face, put it right here in my left hand, and let's get back to smiling and laughing."

It is in these moments that I realize my quality of life is important; Xavier, it matters a great deal to him to see me smile and to hear me laughing. And he does all of this while being non-verbal. When it happens, it's so magical, I will even go as far as to call it spiritual, because the place that it puts me, the place that it takes us to, is so special. It is a place that is only occupied by Xavier and I, and in that place, only he and I exist. The most important thing to us is where we are and keeping the smile on each other's face and hearing us laugh in unison is the most important thing to each of us. For both of us, in this space, time does not exist because while we are there, we have no place to be except where we are at that time. As the song says, "no more troubles of the world." So whatever was bothering me, whatever I was thinking about that put wrinkles in my forehead and took away my smile and silenced my laughter, it has to go. It cannot be allowed in Xavier and my special place. And when it does come, it is all waved away when Xavier extends that massive left hand as if to say, "Put your troubles in my hand," because I am taking us back to that place where we were smiling, to that place where we are smiling—yes, back to that place where Xavier and I are happy.

I always surrender to Xavier and that massive left hand, and to our special place where only he and I exist. And trust me when I tell you this, it is a nice place to be.

Going back to the quote and so many other clichés like "opposites attract," I sometimes wonder how a body like Xavier's houses so much love, how peace is so much a part of who he is, and his spirit is calming, caring, and so not intimidating as his physical presence would convey. So, you really cannot judge this book by its cover, and you cannot put Xavier in a box when it comes to what he can and cannot do. He will surprise and surpass whatever limited expectation that society has put in place for Xavier and anyone else on the spectrum that is on this journey.

So, having said that, I can without a doubt say that we exist as a spirit and we are housed by our body, which brings me to my original thought by Edmund Spenser, which was borrowed from the Greek philosopher Aristotle: "FOR OF THE SOUL THE BODY FORMED DOTH TAKE FOR SOUL IS FORMED AND DOTH THE BODY MAKE" – in my humble opinion, anyway.

Coming to this revelation, I have also concluded that along this journey of being a man of faith, and for a period of time not believing in a higher power (stupidly, I might add), I have been reintroduced to the higher power who is "THE GREAT I AM, MY LORD AND SAVIOR JESUS CHRIST, MY FATHER GOD."

When I was a first grader back in 1968 at an elementary school called Hooper Renwick, my first-grade teacher's name was Miss Camp. She walked with a limp and had kind of a strange disposition about herself. She came off as a disciplinarian, or if you're a child, you would have called her mean. However, for whatever reason, she was nice to me, and she made a great and lasting impression on me, and apparently I made one on her as well. Because years later, as life would have it, I walked into a neighborhood convenience store, and the name of the store was Camp's Grocery. I was twenty-four years old at the time, and I had not seen Miss Camp since I was six years old, which at this time is eighteen years. As soon as she saw me, she said, "Samuel Hutchins! How are you doing?" And I said, "Hello, Miss Camp, how are you?" And she was pleased that I remembered her, and I was equally surprised that she remembered me. She made reference to the time that I won a bookmark for remembering a Bible quote and that I was the only one in her class to remember it or memorize it, and it was John 3:16: "FOR GOD SO LOVED THE WORLD THAT HE GAVE HIS ONLY BEGOTTEN SON AND WHO SO EVER BELIEVETH IN HIM SHALL NOT PERISH BUT HAVE EVERLASTING LIFE."

Okay, two things here. This was 1968, just before desegregation, so Black schools usually ran from first grade all the way to the twelfth grade, and it was okay to mention or have the Bible in the classrooms. It was, however, in 1962, the Supreme Court ruling, Engel v. Vitale, ruled that school-sponsored prayer was unconstitutional. So technically, you could say I started breaking the law in 1968, but I digress. For Miss Camp to make reference to that particular time in her life and how proud of me she was that day, and when I completed my purchase, she took her hands and put them around my hand as I held my bag and she said, "Don't ever forget me." And I replied, "Yes, ma'am." And she said, "Such a gentleman, take care," and I said, "You do the same."

So the Bible has always been a part of my life in a very important way, and in my opinion, everyone should have a favorite verse or a go-to scripture that puts them in a place of reverence. For me, it is Ecclesiastes Chapter 1, Verse 18, and what it basically is stating is that "HE WHO INCREASES KNOWLEDGE ALSO INCREASES SORROW."

Now, all my life, reading has been a hobby or a habit I liked and enjoyed, and the ability to read something and to apply it to your life or see yourself in a particular writing or story was something that always fascinated me. And to read something from years ago and how it still pertains to this time set as it did in some cases hundreds of years ago, and you cannot help but wonder how profound it was at the time it was being written and how it is still profound years later. For me, that is what I call timeless, because when it was written or said is the least important thing in its profoundness. Like the place Xavier and I go to, there is no time, there is no place, it is just us, Xavier and I, and we are just there.

Another quote that had a profound impact on my life was by another Greek philosopher, Heraclitus, and it goes, "Man never crosses the same river twice, for it is not the same river and he is not the same man." This is one that really resonated with me, and for the longest time, I could not figure out why. And then, as they like to say, life starts to "lifing," and then all the "whys" are brought together, and the "ifs" become more of your mental makeup, and you find yourself suspended in time, in thought, and in a place that you are not familiar with. Your hopes and dreams, all of your plans made, and the dreams that you dreamed are questioned and, in some cases, doubted.

I got a call on November 5th from Xavier's biological mother, stating that she and Xavier were out and that Xavier had a seizure and fell headfirst onto the concrete. As a result of the fall, Xavier broke his C5 vertebra, causing paralysis from the neck down. He was rushed to one of the top spinal cord injury hospitals here in the state of Georgia. They operated to repair the vertebra to take the pressure off of the spine, which had been pinched but not severed, so there was still a chance that once the swelling went down, the paralysis would subside and feelings would come back into his arms and legs. So, with the surgery being deemed "successful," it became a waiting game, and so began the healing process.

On day three after the surgery, Xavier began to move that massive left hand, and of course, we were all ecstatic and enthused. Two days later, he had hand movement in his right hand, and so now we have movement in both arms. Now, physical therapy is being talked about, and placement in the spinal clinic for rehabilitation is being talked about and set up. Xavier is showing improvement daily. Xavier and I are doing our nose kisses, and Xavier came up with a game where he would motion for me to cover him up with a blanket, and he would gather the blanket and throw it on the floor. I would pick the blanket up and put it back on him, and he would throw it on the floor and smile.

Then, on day nineteen of being in the ICU unit, Xavier's vital organs started shutting down one by one. First, it was his small intestine; it had died, and part of the large intestine had died also. So the doctors gave us this news, and I was still holding on to my faith. The doctors said that Wednesday morning, they would go back in and remove the dead part of the large intestine, put Xavier on dialysis because his blood was septic and poisoned his bloodstream because his kidneys had shut down. At this time, we were informed that there was a great chance that Xavier would not survive the surgery.

We were asked about a DNR, and if his heart stopped, we agreed to resuscitate him with chest compressions, to give him every chance at life. So they came in on that Wednesday morning, around 10 AM, and prepared him for surgery. Around 11:20 AM, I heard a scream the likes of which I had not heard since my mom went out to see why I couldn't wake my father up after she had sent me out multiple times prior. It was Xavier's biological mom. She had gone to use the bathroom, and as she walked out, she could see the doctors giving Xavier chest compressions. Upon hearing the scream, I rushed to the operating room and was met by a nurse who asked me if I wanted them to continue the chest compressions. I said, "Of course, continue!" However, it was to no avail. Xavier passed at 11:20 AM on November 27th, 2024, just 11 days past his 32nd birthday, which was November 16th.

Numbers, numbers can be an interesting concept. For example, 22 is the number of days Xavier was in ICU, and 22 is also my favorite number. 32 is the age of Xavier when he passed; it is also the age of my dad when he passed. And so, the fourth scar was formed. It has become part of who I am and what I am. The purpose and reason for all that I have, all that I wanted, all that I needed, was now gone. So now, without Xavier, for me, there is no place to take me away from the troubles of the world.

That magical place that Xavier and I shared is no longer there. I grew to love and understand and care in ways I never knew were possible, and I learned and experienced that love and felt it so much and needed it everyday. If you have not experienced or loved someone like I loved my son Xavier, then you are truly missing out on what life really is about, what life can teach us if we are willing to learn.

So now comes the question: What now? What next? What do I do with all these emotions, all of these questions? I now need guidance because I am now in a situation that I was never prepared for. You see, I am thirty years older than Xavier, and in the circle of life, adults are not supposed to bury our children; they are supposed to bury us, because that's what we understand, that's what we expect. So I never envisioned a time that I would be here on this earth without Xavier. My concern had always been Xavier here without me. When I awakened at that hospital, sleeping on the floor, getting up at 7 AM that morning, I had no idea my son was going to die that day. So I find myself where I found myself in two "ready or not" situations.

But then I had to remember who I serve. I had to remember who is the author and finisher of my fate, and I had to remind myself who is the greatest at taking something that was meant for bad and turning it into good. I will tell you, it is THE GREAT I AM, THE PRINCE OF PEACE. And I got to thinking more spiritually, more with my soul, and I am coming to the conclusion that nothing in this world will ever harm Xavier's spirit, because it is his spirit that taught us all we know about autism. It was his spirit that took he and I to that special place where only he and I existed. As his older sister would say after observing us and not realizing she had entered the room, she said, "Y'all two be in y'alls own little world." And I did not realize it at the time, but Carlitha was 100% right. It had always been Xavier's spirit that made us love him like we did. No one's love for Xavier was better than the other; it was just different. And Xavier had everything he needed from us in this world while he was creating for us a life without him. So the earth has his body, God has his soul, but Xavier and his spirit will live on in us as long as we live and until we see him again.

The Xavier Journey Podcast, the Hope 4 Xavier Foundation, the Xavier Duran Hutchins Memorial Hope Park will all have his spirit represented in their existence. Now I am not going to tell you that I understood or that I understand God and how God works. His reasonings are not like ours. God's thoughts are not like ours. And yet, while I don't understand God, I will continue to trust God. I will continue to believe God, because God always has a plan, and none of what any of us go through is a surprise to God. He goes before us, and in this instance, there is a place on this earth for the peace I will need to get to. So the life and legacy of Xavier Duran Hutchins, "The Big Dirty," "Zay," and of course, "Stinkem," will live on. This is his journey.